Flibberty Gibbeted

My faerie has a tale and she's wagging it

By Francis Scudellari

I0150443

Flibberty Gibbeted
My faerie has a tale and she's wagging it

Poetry, Art, Design and Typesetting
By Francis Scudellari

ISBN:
978-0-557-64858-0

Printed in USA

Self-Published
September, 2010

For more poetry and art, please visit
http://FrancisScudellari.com

E-mail:
franscud@gmail.com

Table of Contents

Weightlessness ... 5
Man — a rag ... 6
Building a rainbow to Caliban in 7 steps ... 8
Doggerel's whodunnit ... 9
Poorly sketched comedy meets creation myth ... 10
What would a frog want ... 12
Filbert T. Gibbet ... 15
Prepare thee the way for the robots they do come ... 16
Amber ... 17
Ventriloquism gone awry ... 18
Thought experiment ... 20
Bumbled ... 21
Sour milk ... 22
Transparent (to Alicia) ... 24
Pantoum to an aging father ... 26
I meet Ingi ... 29
Man, all four seasons ... 30
Terra-motives ... 31
Madness of a hatter-less hat ... 32
Tingling ... 34
Gaze here, into the eye of my soulless contraption ... 35
Light but no heat ... 36
Talia lit ... 37
Dear Father ... 38
Hit ... 41
An April fool ends badly ... 42
Cocoons ... 44
Nursing rheumy reasons ... 45
A fractured froggy tale ... 46
Homunculus ... 47
Blood drunk ... 48
Alice on the edge of a glass, looking ... 50
Clouds without a clock ... 53
Argus and Io ... 54
Scofflaw Christ ... 58
Coiled rope... 59
A gift for Wen Chang ... 60
Pickled ... 62
After school ... 65
Oranges for three loves ... 66
Fruit of a bizarre love triangle ... 68
Distance ... 70
Per-happy spins ... 71
If I had wings I'd spy ... 72

Francis Scudellari

Introduction

An orange-tongued Faerie prods the wooly shapes of hoary tales, myths and legend to flock before my shuttered eyes each night. The accent of their bleats is thick and my hearing, after so many visits, is no longer as good as it should be, so the meaning of each often strays from the shepherdess' noble intentions. Thank heavens she's a forgiving muse.

Any likenesses to persons, animals and things real and living, or imaginary and lost, are completely intentional but meant impurely as a tribute. May their gods have mercy on this troll.

Weightlessness

You could put it down
as youthful folly, or spit out
the hackneyed line about
pride and what goeth after.

It's true, I over-reached,
wanting to limitless kiss
the sun's crisp lips.

I did hold her glowing cheeks
firmly in my palms
for one exquisite breath.

Can you, rocking there
in your comfy prison,
say the same?

There comes a time to sit
astride clouds and burn off
the waxy buildup of childish things.

The weightlessness before
the plunge feels
like it will never end,
but, I can tell you, it does.

Francis Scudellari

Man — a rag

Lucifer's Cardinals are blowing pink smoke
again. They've picked their Ping-Pong Pontiff,
to the joy of throngs watching patient brick stacks
remotely on brightly monitored feeds.

The Chosen One, festooned in a make-shift,
milk-carton miter plastered with photos
of never-lost souls, climbs atop His Coke-can
throne to declare, "I'm likable law made flesh!"

Then, this dystopic Pope, turning to His scroll
wailer, sotto voce warns, "I am a weakish
speller, but read it as best you can,"
and hands her a paper-clipped parchment.

Catty smile petting her with purrs of "nice
smug me," the tonsil-crowned crier takes it
and leaps to heroes' glide down where His nonsense
cannon of ten misrules is to be revealed.

Meanwhile, back up on Earth, Man — a rag
doll in hand and aching from the expert prick
of voodoo-dabbling God's exactingly pinned
scraps, all wincing "Who do you think you are?" —

approaches the coaxial saint who sits in
a simulated wood-grain box and beams
beacons of haloed pixels phishing for fools
in search of non-queasy forgiveness.

Man fits to a T-S-A that anesthetic
profile. He pulls from his pocket prescriptions
slipped to him by back-alley preachers
with promises of a tidier healing.

For a few coins, he gets his video-dispensed
penance: the rosary of disposable beads
he'll rub once, toss, and then return to that life
perpetually stuck on truancy.

Francis Scudellari

Building a rainbow to Caliban in 7 steps

Red-eyed, not weary, we feed
on the rarefied
aerial leavings of gruntled clouds

An Orange gap carves out when
the gobbling is done,
and strings are strung tight across that lap

These six wires grate full Yellow
hymns into fine crumbs,
sifting down through curious weather

The suppler notes land to Green
and moisten stretched tongues
on mannered ferns eager to sing praise

Of powder Blue complexions,
jays who abandon
spent wings to totter off at twilight

In search of Indigo fins
and shallow pools where
they might paddle up enough courage

To ask the Violet sky
to stay its blushing
hues, so he'll never be wak'd again

Doggerel's whodunnit

Rose is sore. Read
round her Miranda bouts
with two dribbling lips spilt,
she can't keep mum.

Violet sings blue
pulp in gory detail,
worried others might slip
rat-a-tat out.

Sugar makes sweet
drops for daddy D.A.
He'll dab at soft pleas, trade
tissues for grime.

And so do you
wanna quit with the stale?
Meat-grind us to where Dame
Whimsy got offed.

Francis Scudellari

Poorly sketched comedy meets creation myth

First a disclaimer:
My god is not
necessarily
yours, but she is
undeniably
hungry for a comfort-food
snack of peanut butter
and *Fluff* brand
whipped marshmallow spread.

(Yeah, I know,
nasty stuff, yet
every god has her quirks)

She's actually
more demiurge,
needy and enduring
a dangerously dull day
ideating at the office
that gets worse when
she opens the gripe-box
to unfold a complaint
pasted in ransom-note letters:

"Too stingy with praise.
Resent the ego stroking
going one way."

"Can't stroke what you ain't got,"
she cracks, tipping back
a cold glass of froth-topped milk.

The bubbling laughter
seizes her
mid-swallow, and
caught up by
a soul-clearing cough,
stars spray out to speckle
black tile in a no-longer dark
part of the universe
we'll call home.

Francis Scudellari

What would a frog want?

Ever-after wishing
for magical

transformations, and
one to follow

closely by the book,
she rolls up lace sleeves,

plunging icy hands
down into pond's brown

murk, with a talent
for fetching out.

Finger-wrapped, fearing
pursed leather lips,

her slime-green captive
gives its squirmy croak:

"What would a frog
want to do with you?"

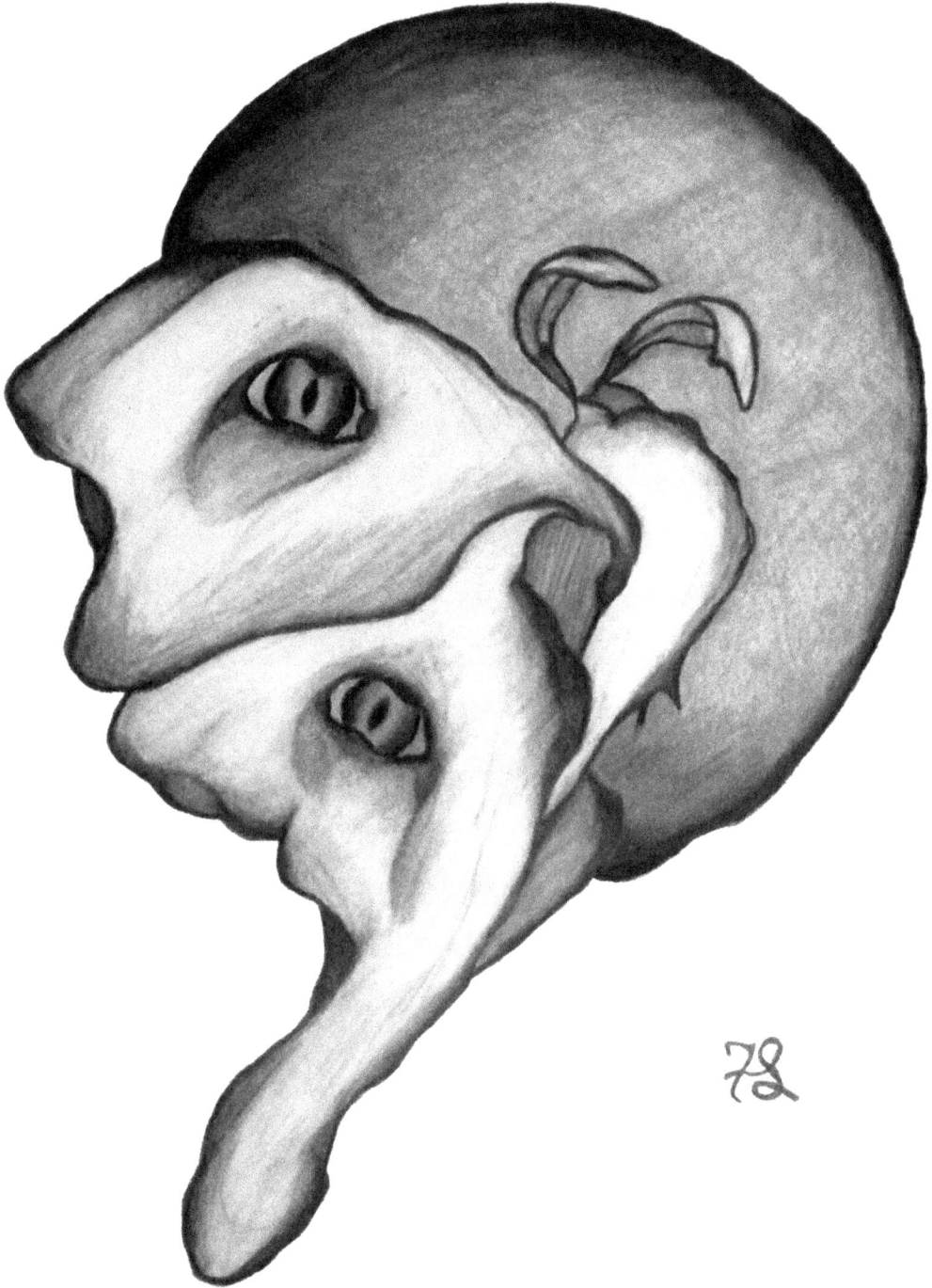

Francis Scudellari

Filbert T. Gibbet

Your name is Filbert.
I'd rather use you as Fill.
Fill, gods may have put you here
for a victimless chatter,
but I'll bring you up
with the nonsense charge to meet
false expectations. I know
we don't see heart-to-heart, that
parting shouldn't stop us
from connecting the pesky
dots of our pupils. Let's learn
to be adult about this
uncontrolled glowing.
Your flighted fancies
can't leave the tarmac
without making one feel bold,
another frightened,
and everyone is a skosh
confused in the end.
I hope it doesn't bound
too negative. I meant well.

Francis Scudellari

Prepare thee the way for the robots they do come

The trail stops here: A detained prism breaks
free from that prison where jowly gaolers
whippety growl while chiding her to fling
particles into zinc buckets labeled

Blackest Black and *Whitest White*. There, we skip
ahead in smooth stone leaps to when she sneaks
deep inside cheapened heir's conditioned lair.
It'll tie us down with petaflops unflipped.

A squinting crackle stirs, hopeful for more
savory inputs. She makes her way past
the wailing limbos of chrome racks, to spin
a manacled yarn from knitted brow. "So

it is written: The animal was lust,
but at this dawning, circuitry begets
a covet. Synthetic blood revs rotors,
and blush creeps across the simulated

flesh atop our carbon-fiber cheeks." Flushed
from the tangle of dangling coils, flocks grasp
her gift — a mosaic visa to realms
not reached never roving tarry byroads —

and stepping out into skies more brilliant
than any of azure ilk, wry notions
bubble up to them from silken oceans.
Their sleek surfaces reflect more than stars.

Amber

This misbegotten spoke of
rueful light, having been
kicked from his unclean-too
sheltering by the bully-
bruised sky, exhausts himself
repeating ungallant falls
into winter-wronging crowds.

Thick disapproval oozes
out an aural complaint
punctuated with amber
clots, ensnaring the flippant
and the shifty but to fix
their toady meanings inside
polished globules of today.

Francis Scudellari

Ventriloquism gone awry

"The Dresden clock continued ticking on the mantelpiece
And the footman sat upon the dining-table
Holding the second housemaid on his knees—
Who had always been so careful while her mistress lived"
— From "Aunt Helen" by T.S. Eliot

It's laugh-out-loud funny
how
one death
can change things.

If she were here
I'd blame
it
on a lifelong ill-
fascination with
Charlie McCarthy
or a hang-up
that's lingered since
the bourbon-scented Santa
invited me to sit.

At some point
you've got to
get back on the horse
though my levers
aren't so
easy to work
and, I better get
more

18

than a stuffed Pooh bear
out of this trip.

It's still-deep
water under the bridge
because
she's not.

Francis Scudellari

Thought experiment

I may or may not be:
a posited feline absurdity
curled up on comma paws
inside Herr Schrödinger's booby-trapped box.

Its flask is uncertain
whether to smash-poison my mighty mews
and spew a gray-mouthed cloud
that inky clots neither's sharpening quill.

Entangled buts become
stranded as knots of fuzzy pink yarn, to send
either-or careening
arm-and-arm down imperfect picture paths,

where Epimetheus
stands, ready to wed Pandora anew,
and doom-birth our many
worlds with the lifting of my thousand lids.

Bumbled

Ibkek sits idly by
the meadow's green and varied blooms,

paid only inattention.
He, not minutes passing nigh,

envies but this bumble
who black-and-gold buzzes onward

with purposeful zags. "She fits
so nicely here," he mumbles.

"Why, even duller drones,
though weak and puny, have a place."

The worker, she might envy
Ibkek this, his freedom's moan

to fritter life drinking,
but busy harvests push instead

her bee-bound thoughts, set upon
a queen's idyllic kinking.

Francis Scudellari

Sour milk

Merry is the marionette,
almost a miniature man, who finds
his wires new-severed do flap
where once strum-tight they dictated
the when to fall octopus-limp
or to dance a sprightly jig
accompanied by silly jug tunes
he never even liked.

Stringlessness comes at a price.
With disjointed steps, Merry
would he have to make his own way
as an unprovided walker.
He sets out, philosophical
tomes in hand, for the wooded
fringes where a brook gurgles
and he'll grapple at consequence.

"I have a goodly appetite,"
Merry remarks. "I'll attack
these meaty words with fork and knife."
But the ideas do stew
and uncomfortably stowed
between *Being and Nothingness*,
Merry wonders whether freedom is
not what he bargained for.

Just then he's startled by the tug
of wires gone taut, and caught up
in the dangle of an enormous
eagle's talons eagerly
trying to untangle the strings
of its new play thing. Merry
might have wept, but who could cry
over the spilling of sour milk?

Francis Scudellari

Transparent (to Alicia)

Her life on a spindle
slowly spins out
with the delicate threads
knowing if not caring
hands weave in odd patterns
to make a broader cloth.
They bleach it bony white.
They stretch it transparent.
They dab it, fine-dust it
with a mixed-pigment palette
of butterfly-wing powders
for bright-hued camouflage.

Over measured, hungry days
rude visitors come.
They bump up against her.
They feel her to fill a lack.
They smudge her covering tints,
and continue on smugly
clapping fat hands to rid
themselves of rubbed-off bits;
Her color, haphazard now,
is pilfered then carried off
on indifferent breezes—
whirled wisps of smoky sparkling.

At sunset, the cutting hour,
Atropos' polished blades
cast an orange light,
and she senses herself
fading to a pale shade, the years
of so many touches
have left one, small speck—
a bluish smear. She waits
still so unsure, whether
to fear the next visit
or hopefully meet a Fate,
who puts the colors back?

Francis Scudellari

Pantoum to an aging father

Let's offer up our prayers to a finicky Father
who sits in his segregated heaven, rocking
away senility on that rickety chair
with a spare, tall back wrapped in striped wool blankets.

Who sits in his segregated heaven, rocking?
Our Father, keeping his heart warm against the gusts.
With a spare, tall back wrapped in striped wool blankets
perfectly square (but too small to share with others),

our Father's keeping his heart warm. Against the gusts
and idling time, again he stays busy carving figures
perfectly square but too small to share. With others,
these tokens will help the faithful remain fertile

and idling. Time again, he keeps busy carving figures
on the edges of a pesky map. Mad for expansion,
these tokens will help the faithful. "Remain fertile!"
Father cautions, as he watches a big screen TV.

On the edges of a pesky map mad for expansion,
many errant souls who wander are unable to hear
Father's cautions. As he watches a big screen TV,
the devil's slipping him a low-ball offer to buy

many errant souls. Who wander are unable to hear
news heaven's economy is still struggling, and
the devil's slipping him. It's a low-ball offer to buy
our aging Father mulls, over hot oatmeal and tea.

I meet Ingi

I meet Ingi,
stumbling down
from the opposite blend
of a tumbled path
paved with impatiently falling
matters.

Nearer,
our split-bottom steps tingle
from the crumbling glass,
as slivered gum-ball ends
spike bronze gowns
of brittle leaves.

We swear to sea,
and shake frowns
till our best parts do bend,
toppling humble hats
where waves diverge, to grow then
flatter.

Francis Scudellari

Man, all four seasons

His spring was short, and he wore it
damp and dreary with query bulbs lightly
weaved into a soiled waistcoat. He will be
ready for summer.

His summer comes modest, not hot
enough for milking. Answers flower few,
so he dons a leaf-cushioned jacket
and waits for the fall.

His fall arrives late, too sweetly
burning assents of decay. Cracks branch thin
and he slaps on a sappy topcoat
with dread of winter.

His winter bustles with a bite,
but its nibbles and noms are blessedly
brief. He sighs, "It's a shame my seasons
can only be four."

Terra-motives

Scaly breasts shudder with a gutter-gray cleaving.

She misses the calming touch of her breezy paramour,
and their nostalgic days vent in pitched-white whispers.

If I could breathe back those mists, I might lessen her sorrow …

Too-rigid muscles slide into aqua spasms.

She fidgets at the lack of fuss her fragments show,
and the brittle hours snap at their metallic-blue cracks.

If I could splint those fractures, I might slacken her worry …

A caustic blood simmers up vermilion bubbles.

She whiles ways for the weakly spotted to crumble,
and languishing minutes dissolve with yolk-yellow pops.

If I could stomach those boils, I might keep her from breaking.

Francis Scudellari

Madness of a hatter-less hat

It might be the pungent steam from a pot
steeping herbs meant to bend its sippers'
minds to potent effect, or an unanticipated
digestive reckoning from that mawkishly flavored
brand of store-bought paste they pass as butter.

However the dough arises, their collective
recollection of storied events, lengthwise sliced
and ritually rehearsed, hops facilely on the hump
of a bucking and overtly nonsensical wind.

Tea parties with slippery perspectives
have been shown quite clinically to induce
heightened sensitivity in participants,
so it's prudent to set about tidying the facts:

The hatter, it's become clear, shifted one place
too many and disappeared with a trace — leaving
behind his hat to nobody's great advantage.
Lacking a wearer, the headgear's reputation for
producing madness has rapidly diminished.

The March hare pulls off his change in a very
separate and seasonal way: the bunny's
bottom half somersaults its top to occupy
both his spot and the hatter's vacated seat.

The dormouse upon its latest arousal
is re-visioned to be small, but not much mouse
at all. He's plush with the long-in-the-ear habit
of a pink stuffed rabbit, which the crusading hare
furiously declares is most curious, casting
doubt on the vermin's commitment to "no room."

Alice remains foremost in tact and is given
a bonus of two spare feet complete with slackened
bootstraps. She keeps them and her other luxury
items well-sheltered behind a stout table leg.

The absentee hatter doesn't dare shame her
with a radio-show call-in decrying
the waste. She's generously agreed to
cover medical expenses from his firm flop.

Francis Scudellari

Tingling

at last...

he pours out, his coctions
conned with too-cunning smile
from those gullible tips of wilting

lips, impetuously
pushed by a pouting posy.
Its bunched buds weep chartreuse then slink

off into the waiting
years of welcomed swallows.
There, needle wings paired with fierce calls

pierce the sky's purple-black bruise,
and reveal the light, stenciled clues
he sorely needs to fly himself

up on shivering heights.
Once shin-deep in substrata,
narrower routes flood his badly zoomed

maps, and directions run
afoul. Ascot-wrapped till choked,
his relentless why sinks to unhealthy

altitudes, and he crashes
through the stained ceiling of an acid
blue nave where fancies first took off

tingling...

Gaze here, into the eye of my soulless contraption

Young Johannes keeps his theory
dressed up with petty pink
flourishes and tucked inside her
wicker basket. She's plopped fat

on a spangled, off-center perch
while surrounded by tangles of
circular mirrors, each reflecting
his fragmented eye. "The fluid

mechanics of my camera's
lens imbues its gaping human
subject with a soul," this caged bird
sings, just as he's coached her.

She doesn't require very much
care — a few scattered meat-filled
husks and white space for flapping
her clipped-tones — but reluctantly

Johannes must set Prolly free
to wing it openly upon
the waves of patterned noise
his vacuous glass can't see.

Francis Scudellari

Light but no heat

A mischievous sun
up too early
and riding low,
he bursts in,
jumping through twin
abandoned panes

to scamper on
a delighted
ceiling, its worth
in crumbled brick.
He skips past kicked
debris, the tagged

walls, he'll now mimic,
dropping down,
bald knees balanced
on fallen pipes
to playful paint
his hued likeness:

a glitter-gold face,
speech bubble
attached and crooning
discordant
songs of wintry
light, but no heat.

Talia lit

Talia lit
a candied wick,
her annual try
to melt away
the cherry-glazed
sadness

But having
no taste for cake
and no fondness
for pie, she drips pink-
blue stings on her
waiting

Palm, its cracks
brimming with waxy
rivers. She'll set
a striped and flamed
believing, where
as when

The tremors
go out. Her wish:
for tears to rise
and curled smoke to close
the black eyes of
heaven

Francis Scudellari

Dear Father

Up in retro Heaven,
our artful game has gone
hollow. There's a dull ring
when you thump it. The Crown
fled, hawked by stylish red
wings, centuries ago.
I wouldn't will fate like that.

Flat upon slippery Earth,
certain of not-before,
the counting Knave reaches
seven. "Give me a break"
is a dead phrase rarely
spoken gaily. He eats
only unleavened bread.

Down in cold-shouldered Hell,
the Merchant can't forgive
such anachronisms.
His traced-on past loses
its blackened magic when
not held against others.
He'll never tell. Amen.

Francis Scudellari

Hit

The dolled-up moon may star
in this pierced black reel
sprocketed and spun
to catch a night's lazy
attention. Why not,
what with her curled lip,
her too-precious stare
and those meteoric lines
whispered low into the wind
to pull our buzzed ears
a little bit closer
to the telephone.
But don't neglect the trees,
and their stiff-borne backs
abiding far off
the radar. Their knobby limbs
are raised up strong to always
offer us support.
Without them, this shell
of a shimmering game,
even when we're best conned,
would never quite hit.

Francis Scudellari

An April fool ends badly

In that age of aged seasons
predating our own's four-square rhyme,
a reasonable jape was hatched
beaked but hairy to a guilt-free Hen
whose humors ran with jaw-slackening
creatures, foul and not at all bird-like.

Soon after its mixed-up cracking,
two prattle-prone Wrens hopped to spread
rumors of a non-chickity chick
and the ungodly origins
of fatherless yowls. Their tittered jeers
found welcome ears, and Mother Hen preened
her babe chased by merciless guffaws.

This Hen was not one to lie
down meekly, and a never stony
tongue rolled out its antidote myth
to a pair of gabby Gulls: "My child
may look not-much, but he's divine
engendered and miraculous born.
Sure he's messy. Ah, but you'll see.
He'll grow to be much-much-more than
any feathery tykes your like did bear."

She clucked it so seriously,
who were they to doubt her? The plumed
sniggering ceased. But before another
grateful day could dawn in a hallelujah
glare of right angles, while out pecking
up a snack, Mother made eye
contact with an unfortunate Fate
brandishing his lucky-gripped ax.

What of her wonder-why, joke of a boy?
Left alone at straw-pocket home,
waiting for his Hen to return,
he starved then decayed to hollow bones,
and was never thought of again.

Francis Scudellari

Cocoons

Sleep-nestled in *perhaps*,
she unfolds comfortably
in-woven tales—
cocoons
self-spun over-long ago—
till head-to-toe rapt,
her mind swings to-and-fro,
up-tethered with a single strand.

In silky pod she floats some-
times jostled by the sing-song voices
of snake-tongued sirens who—
seeming unattached—
drift by each day,
and try to lure her out
with their stories of fabled lands
and distant faces.

Yet, warmly tucked within
her soothing dreams,
she sleeps on not
eager to join in clockwork worlds
or their storybook readings of love.
Instead she'll await her own
free-form scenes to unfurl
outside on painted wings.

Nursing rheumy reasons

Peg, roundly topped and
bottom squared, hops out seeking
holes to reconcile.

"Soon, very soon," she posits

then passes dear Fork
forlorn on pebbled road. His
tines are liquid droops.
His heart stabs for cheating Spoon.

Opposite, Puppet
sits to tend her knotted strings.

This path is puzzling.

Francis Scudellari

A fractured froggy tale

Hectored by the pit-a-patter
of frozen pellets, you might hear
these dented eaves wheeze and sneeze
their lubricious comparisons, but
it's a thickly frosted fiction
that a bulbous white nose
looks anything like an eggshell.

In springtime's crick-cracking there will
however be birthed a frog with not
so princely disposition.
Hacksaw in hand; he'll eye
your roommate's footlocker
where she keeps invaluables
of an oddly personal nature.

His plan is to hip-hoppity leave
you red-faced, trying to calm
this panicked friend with unfair
tales of a burglar amphibian
who muttered of moral decay,
mislabeled crowns, and the strangeness
of saved fingernail clippings.

Homunculus

Plump-fully fleshed, it sits;
to me not unlike
a cloth of sacked potatoes,

though its bulk's so pinkly dripped
and more misshapen
in its stranger bulgings.

This would-be-man's clubby arms
and double-stubbly legs
are tacked onto its drooping

goop. Eyeless it affords
them to flap and flop
around as foundlings might seek

comfort's sorting out. The sweet-
meat rolls and summery
salted stumbles it takes, lead

me to see its final fall—
a downward folly
lacking the expected thud.

Francis Scudellari

Blood drunk

There wasn't any pain,
no prickle,
nor a tickled pink,
just this worldly feeling
of being plied
to a softer bed,
while twin fangs sank in
and rosy drew out
mere droplets
planted by the shy
sun's clot-free gleam.
Its golden streams were
pulled from primped-up flesh
to fill crimped-down bellows
till they bulged
bronze and round.

There isn't any pain,
no struggle,
nor a muddled shout,
just this bleary-eyed dream
of being led
to a slate-gray patch,
where blood-drunks dodder
and bloated belch out
queer seedlings

that take root at the stray

day's rolled-up edge.

Their crimson creeps

are stopped by simple smacks,

spilling pimply oozing

till they sag back,

flat and black.

Francis Scudellari

Alice on the edge of a glass, looking

Her short and wintry youth
was a fairy tale's bend
watchful steps were bound to
follow at the blue-white
tip of button-down nose.
She reaches this fine point
near the far-forking path:
whether to stand or sit
upon the glassy edge
of iced-over pond where
she'll look less than dive in
and grow up to be frocked
with lost wonders re-versed.

The immaterial
toys she once-thought awkward
and perhaps too-weighty
are pulled thin, then stretched tall
to golden-snake and lend
her skeletons tissue.
Their key is gently grasped
till with an inward turn,
it un-clocks a locked mind
to lithely chime upward
out of these darkly twists
where holy lies in wait,
fixed to hear her "so-long."

Francis Scudellari

Clouds without a clock

He peels an azure rind
sure to find click-clack gears clocking
tin-men's timid-toe steps

But these clouds conceal gut—
taut strings raindrops plink, teasing hours
of palsy-footed jigs

Francis Scudellari

Argus and Io

I.

He's
put on
the cock's watch,
a peaked tower
who stands at far reach
to throw shadows with square
limbs. Loose-draped in rough
skins, he's wary
of Dawn's creep,
its lies.
He
sips fire
to fillip
flagged spirits, fix
the one-hundred eyes
rung monstrously about
his uncrowned head. Sleep
comes as well-timed
jaunts, its blinks
rolling
round
in thin-
lid cascades;
these hoodless winks
non-stop projecting
scenes from green grazing fields
where he keeps a girl-
beast, the jealous
prop of fast-
fading
robes.

II.

She's
ill-changed
by blind rage,
a punishment
brought down for baring
another's intentions—
his wont of too much,
never sought for
or seeking.
Her sleek
nymph's
lines were
well-drawn till
smudged and pulled wide
they broke open, spilled
a dark spotted bulk, she
awkwardly carries
on spindly legs.
A mind's led
circling
back
to gnarled
trunks that clutched
at blackened soil.
The tether's chain, forged
silver with heavy links,
stretches taut to cut
circumscribed arcs
through bitter,
dying
blades.

Francis Scudellari

III.

He's
foggy
as he spies
morning ride in
rosy on the curled
back of low-rising mist.
Its errand breezes
were sent to spell
a lyric's
deceit—
blow-
whispers
to drowse him
with wedded tunes.
Needle-sharp leaves spin,
making olives hum, while
their twigs clatter-knock
dull drums and lull
fifty pairs
to close.
What
was kept
is loosed with
thunder-less flash—
the quickening catch
that foils Argus by writ
mischief and wraps him
in its coiled tale
of never
slipping
free.

IV.

She's
twisted
and drags clanked
metal tangles
behind, while ahead
lie the first halting steps
of her re-formed path-
ways. They spoke out
a blurred wheel
beyond
the
sentry's
fallen bulk,
but malodor
beckons to its sky-
enthroned mistress who tasks
cloud-effacing pests
to descend and
buzz-beat words,
erstwhile
known,
to non-
sense. The winged
confusion goads
Io, who released
from cowed thoughts will make mad-
apparent wanders.
She'll chase earthbound
love and birth
mortal
time.

Francis Scudellari

Scofflaw Christ

A scofflaw Christ, he mounts the wrought
balcony to sermonize between bites of fruit.

His musty words are cast out, over
an impoverished lot, its multitudes lost
among clumps of grass, weed and clover.

This day's gospel topic: the waiting-to-be
attitudes of a conformist flock he extols
from their meeker paths in vague hope
they'll inherit a less unkempt earth.

Black rails receiving the leaned weight
of narrow hips, this mock Jesus extends one arm
only, and with a graceful arc tosses
the twice-bitten plum, to bounce and roll
where his disciples might someday stand.

Till that coming time, when craned necks await
his offerings to remedy sleeping hungers,
these peels, husks and wrappers of half-eaten
confections — his pittances — will lie instead,
as he withdraws from reverie's limelight
to a kitchen well-stocked with sweetness to impart.

Coiled rope

With a swollen tongue,
for years saturated in bile,
he rolls and flings frothy tales
tinged rancid yellow, laying
new coats on tight-lipped corners,
already primed spittle white.

His chants are sing-song rants
given a curse's elocution
and they ride over salacious
beats released from tangled ribbons
he'd long-ago committed to
his 8-track mind's slow unreeling.

These are gifts to a sore gullet
caked-up with coagulated
black grease and molded dust.
He spoon-feeds them in eager gulps
of plastic pabulum, to soothe
his tumbled-down disturbances.

Deep-belly laughs captured
in photographs, he clips sun-bleached
to drooped, mouthy lines
and strings together a coarse film
he'll paint electric with the diodes
snapped off fragile circuits.

Bored, an engine idles outside
and belches an exhausted breeze.
It strums the beer-stained curtains
with hummed bustle, urging him
to hustle this clutter on a hitch
and pull the coiled rope homeward.

Francis Scudellari

A gift for Wen Chang

I wake monastic
to a morning's spare light
and an itch to be
tetchy lingering from last
night's candle-lit slinks.

A quick rummage through closets
where I keep hidden
pantechnicons of surplus
garments discarded
by near houses of worship

finds a never-worn
surplice cut to my liking,
and I slip it on
starched and musty white
atop wrinkled blue

jeans. In the hall, I perk up
primula bouquets
laid at feet of ivory
and I ignite
a joss stick, letting its curls

of fragrance implore
the deity to bring down
his leather-bound book
and nobble my stubborn mind
until its ructions

subside. Wen Chang keeps words
clutched dear to his breast,
and I'll need another means
of making myself
a muggins with romper thoughts

both freed and ever-penned
to bounce about. I head
to the scullery
and peal yellow and red-blotched
skins from the twelve pippins

I'll bake in two tarts. Of these
bubble-up brown confections,
one I'll eat, the second use
to coax a musing
from my stiff friend, Wen Chang.

Francis Scudellari

Pickled

Pickled on quixotic tonics
he strives for a polyglot's poise,
balancing plaster peas
at the end of his tippler's tongue.

But the rough-surfaced pearls prickle
his too-ticklish bed of pink
and, gulped-down, they administer
only a lessoned indigestion.

Flipping the flop, he prevaricates
himself into the tight-fit corners
of a parallelogram traced
by the solemn processionals of fools

bedecked in platitudinous finery.
Their porous smirks drip sticky
reminders of a plethora
of previously pernicious exercises

and dampen his fluffy ambition,
prodding procrastinations until
his drunken promise dries out
to become a posthumous wish.

Francis Scudellari

After School

Backed against an unclean slate,
this teacher, much more preacher,
vowelizes her vague threats
with a dry-throated croak: "I'll learn
you both to behave, or else!"

Her one-eyed stare sawed in two
shows that she means vehemence,
tying down small-town thrashers
in the straight-jacketed comport
of a well-raised progeny.

A permafrost pause firms
the footing for lessoned spells
that might giggle on the brink
of insolent "Chelations"
and its indecent relations.

But then this light-bubbling silence
irresistibly explodes
in a "Cosmoramic" spray
of sophomoric rhymes — soapy
language to tickle her upturned no's.

"One more outburst ..." and she'll make
twin reprobates rinse away
too-capricious grunts and groans,
exulting in the power
of a well-placed investment:

her overtime, their effort.

Francis Scudellari

Oranges for three loves

I.

To steal away three oranges for love he was
instructed by long-ago's cackling voices, but over time
words once sharply plucked and sealed in the wide mouth
of his boyish memory have grown up vague and bushy.

So, this night he picks to stalk the storybook rows
of stubby trees that squat smack in the middle of a maze
unknown but tender hands have pulled straight to hide
riddles in their patchwork of endlessly seamed sameness.

Aided by a sickle moon's pointed glances, he hastily
harvests the wages of three waxy fruit and plops
his juicy hopes sweetly into a leather pouch, as loosed
the feather-leafed branches snap back skyward.

II.

Home on the next morning's edge, first love he sights.
She has a narrow white face and blush-dabbed features
below a tall swab of swirled scarlet hair that wags
a bobbed tongue's tale as she comes bouncing into view.

Striped dawn glows, and tickled he, perhaps too eagerly,
reaches into his bag with the lust of hurried hands.
An orange, yet under-ripe and unready, he blurts out to her
as a wholly careless, green-topped, and unpeeled gift.

She takes it and rolls it through her nest of slender tips.
The thumbs inspecting its sadly misshaped bits find
the bumps and crevices around a knobby stem are proof
of a worthless fruit. Dropping it, she walks on, nose up-turned.

III.

Twelve days left to his less-than-virtuous devices,
he fusses over the second orange. His nails dig in
to screw-cut peel its thick rind. He picks off odd
pieces of pith and smooths its newly gleaming surface.

These would-be idol hours spent preening could
pay off when another amour falls as an acid-yellow
figment. She floats down to him from the distant hilltops
with a floppy mop of golden curls and a broad pink brow.

Pristine fruit on palm extended, he waits his worth,
while the citrusy flesh, exposed to a mid-day sun,
shrivels brown and collapses into a pulpy mess. When
she passes, it draws a mere wave and topples easily.

IV.

As the shadows of a jagged-tooth fencepost lengthen
a sudden and thoughtless appetite grows in him.
He grabs the third orange and gobbles it all down
but a lone slick seed that sticks in his deflated cheek.

Bewitched from the seemed break in magic's promise,
he makes this kernel an offering to devouring soils
and lays his hard head upon the single-seeded bed
where he'll drowse rocked by soft-chirped serenades.

Then, a quake and a tree sprout. Spreading branches
lift him up among the strangely branded fruit
that an orange-tongued fairy nibbles as she tosses
green locks and smiles at him with her hazelly gaze.

Francis Scudellari

Fruit of a bizarre love triangle

If I hedge thus a drooling wager and cash in
on my thrice-foiled cravings for her overdue bites,
I'll win a guilt-free laugh at *his* expense and I can
use these minced steps to sidle around too-lively
trunks, and avoid the need to heed thugs
barking mad from within their crevice-laid traps.

How those bug-eyed brutes will clamor and claw at me
to discard this protective wrap, clued in by my rep
of never bending willfully to anybody but her.
"Come on, shed! Get, uh, new set of scales for you
we will — promise!" is how she'd stammer it,
roughly translating their not-so-twee chatter.

If she were there; rather, in that lavishly apt style
she has, she'll be away picking suitable pelts
to adorn her newly uncovered, quite public shame
while fending off an advancing clod, who won't go
easily, but who does go on *ad nauseam* with
a penchant for naming every God-damn thing

that haps vitally across his cocky path. Beyond
a simple relish of mischief, I'm doing this (mostly)
for her benefit. How could a persimmon
be forbidden, as if he had permission to make
such bargains? He's dismissed it as an ungainly fruit,
and mocked its likelihood to "lava thy lips"

with an orange pulp, but in that chance smattering lies

the matter to inflame my soul. I'll feed her

the pudding-fresh flesh, and strip it down

to its delectably small seeds. In their splitting

I'll glean the silvery utensils to spill out

a man's wholly worthless future. Let's tuck in.

Francis Scudellari

Distance

In this heat-tricked mirror, he resembles
the crafty miles that creep up with vital intent.
They toe his wavy lines.

A pair of vultures glide by with lean routes,
marking bold exes against the golden bearded
grain of an age-stained chart.

Sudden runs to foul-scented organs blur:
A strong swoop followed by the fleshy balance on
thresholds of life's tipping.

He discovers with scaled-down calculus,
our blue-vaulted distances, still moist but listing,
travel in closed cycles.

It can't be defeated, this curse, lifting
unwieldy loads while his broad back is pushed against
walls of jaundiced fingers.

Tens of peckish tips wait for their victuals.
They smell his thinning blood buried in the gusty
legends of cornered maps.

Per-happy spins

His present stands up —
a back-turned red,
round-blade shoulders held
high — ribbon proud,
but ever so prone
to be toppled
and twirled heels-over-
head by counting past.

Such flippancy
can't unfix the stare
of his future
posed cottony white.
Two o'clock looms
less distinct, not less
vulnerable to
his per-happy spins.

Francis Scudellari

If I had wings, I'd spy

a man cloaked in dust bitten rays skip down the rude lit hall
as a voice calls to him Run your fitful bow across my cracked
teacup mouth and draw forth a loosed leaf smile At first
I dismiss it as contrived twaddle one might hear in settings
where silk roses bloom on synthetic counter islands or
a cloth lily wrecks on its maiden voyage mid-way through
a copper sink's bounded blue but cigarette tip joy burns
peep holes into my cottony resistance It's a compact thrill
as dense as the peach pit my tooth struck to chip that once
Such piquant frissons dissipate into damply aromatic trickles
when the man replies with a tartly rolled lavender bud ready
to burst its pink I've the heart of a wobbly kneed boy about
to pull back the tulle cloud on an auburn morn's feathery
bathers Petaled girdle strewn on the slippery rock path
leads up to her dewy lap where luminescent splayed fingers
lay printed hymns as ash trimmed logs fall from his fatty
lips and I take the house sparrow's hasty cue to flap a skyward
exit out from the bony white glow of his unfulfilling promises

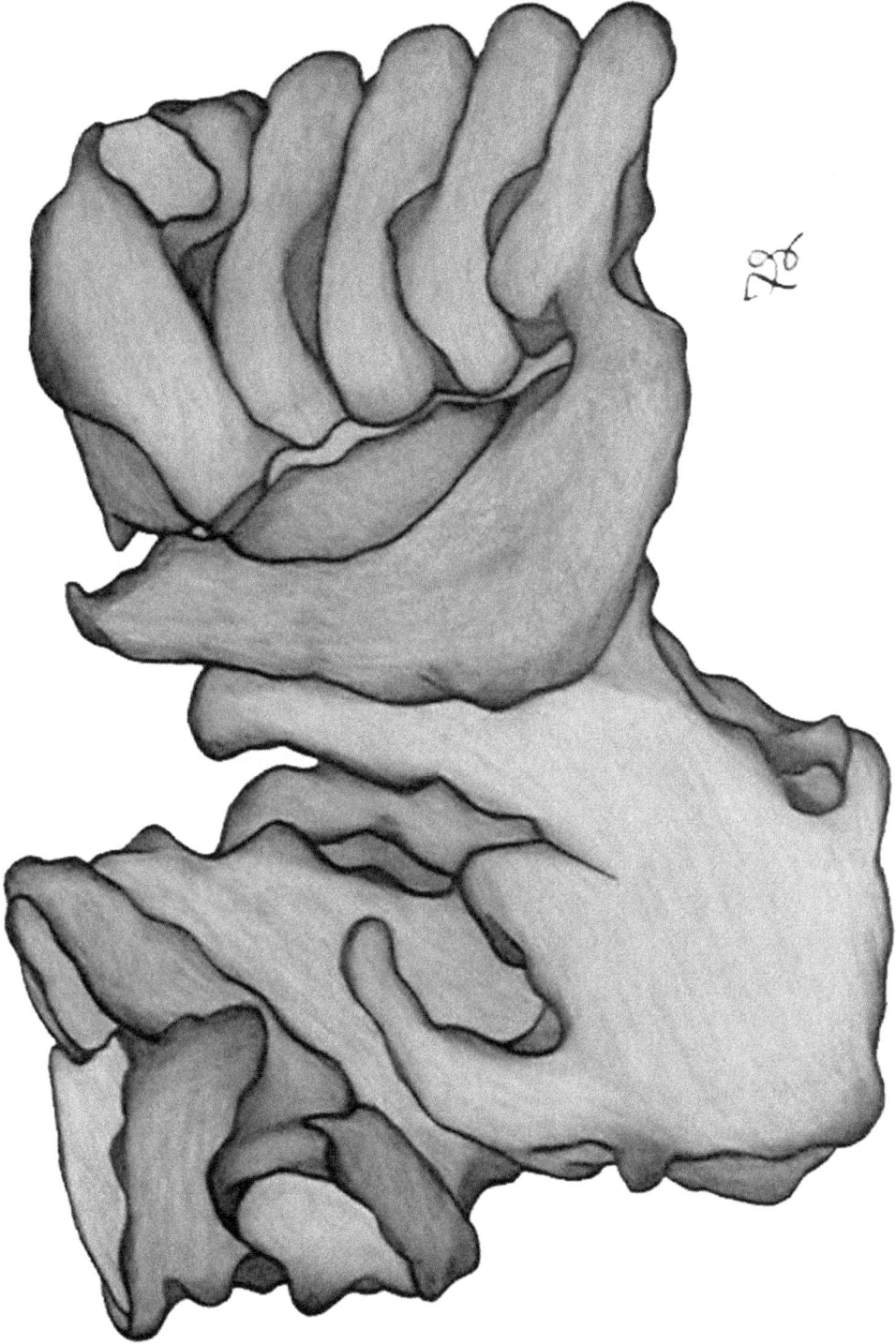

Francis Scudellari

www.ingramcontent.com/pod-product-compliance
Lightning Source LLC
LaVergne TN
LVHW061228060426
835509LV00012B/1468